THE ESSENTIAL
CASABLANCA

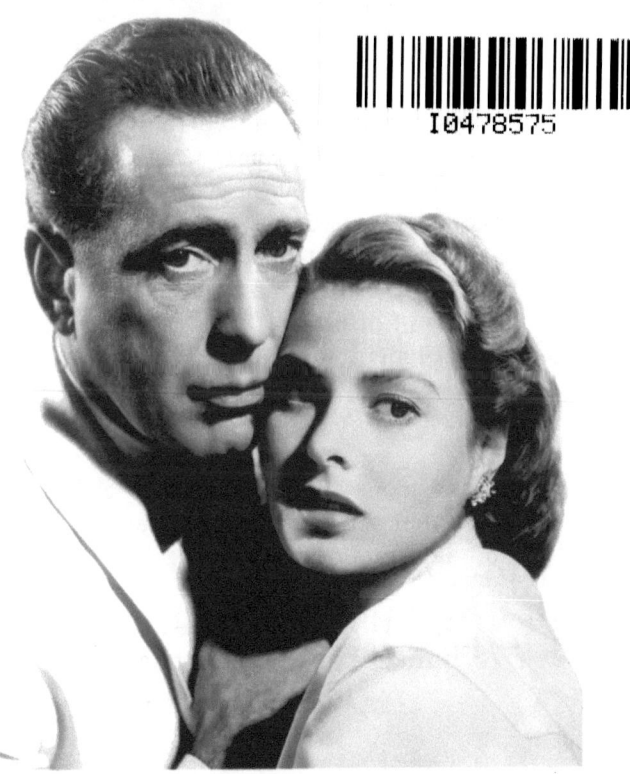

I0478575

101 THINGS YOU DIDN'T KNOW ABOUT AMERICA'S FAVORITE FILM

BY HORACE MARTIN WOODHOUSE
AUTHOR, *THE ESSENTIAL WIZARD OF OZ*

COPYRIGHT NOTICE

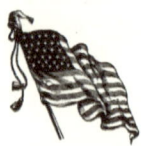

DEDICATION

He is the unsung author of the play on which the iconic film was based. In his play, as in the movie, a thief named Ugarte murders two German couriers for letters of transit that will provide safe passage to Lisbon and the free world. And a mysterious American café owner with a piano-player friend and a crooked roulette wheel bets a womanizing French policeman that a heroic anti-Fascist will escape. To Murray Burnett, who said that Rick was the man he wanted to be, this book is dedicated.

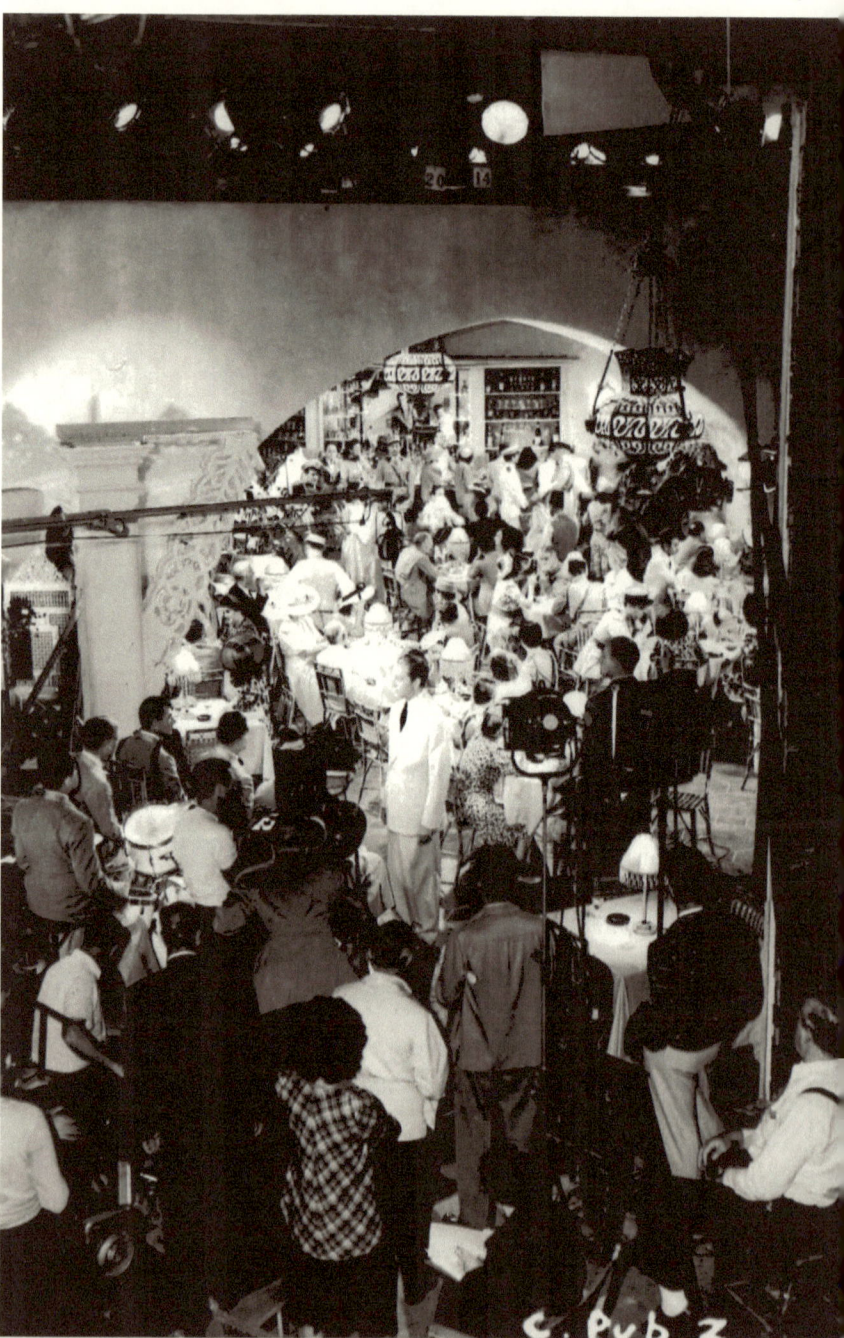

"Casablanca has a life of its own. There is something about it. It seems to have filled a need, a need that was there before the film, a need that the film filled."

— Ingrid Bergman

We'll Always Have *Casablanca.*

In French occupied Morocco during World War II, Rick's Café Americain serves as a way station for expatriates and political refugees. Rick, the cynical saloonkeeper, refuses to take sides with any nationality, but when a former lover and her husband arrive in Casablanca, desperate for visas, he is drawn into a web of politics and romance.

For all of its flaws, inconsistencies, and "loose ends," and perhaps because of them, *Casablanca* gets better every time you watch it. The hastily conceived and executed studio film came together with a cast, director and writers, who by happy accident created a masterpiece of the cinematic art, a venerable piece of filmmaking.

And given its ubiquity in popular culture and its place in the hearts of generations of moviegoers, one wonders, after all this time, if there could be anything more we don't already know about it. No matter how familiar the images, how memorable the lines, how timeless the story, the answer is, yes, there's a whole book worth of things most will be "shocked, shocked" to learn. You're holding that book in your hands.

The Essential Casablanca is brimming with amazing true stories, corrected myths, and particular particulars about the most popular movie in the history of cinema. It's not meant to provide a comprehensive nor com-plete academic reference, but rather an accessible distillation, a delightful confection in its own right, about a film that is one of the most beloved pieces of motion picture art and one that has resonated across nearly three-quarters of a century.

The entries can be read in any order. Randomness is part of the fun; there is no organization, neither alphabetically nor chronologically. Browse through this little book to satisfy your curiosity. It's guaranteed to reveal things you never knew about *Casablanca*.

— Horace Martin Woodhouse

The bittersweet ballad, "As Time Goes By," written by lifelong bachelor Herman Hupfeld, was first performed by Frances Williams in the musical comedy *Everybody's Welcome* which played on Broadway from October 1931 to February 1932.

Hupfeld never wrote a whole Broadway score, but he became known as a composer who could write a song to fit a specific scene within a Broadway show. Other songs by Hupfeld include "When Yuba Plays the Rhumba on the Tuba," "Let's Put Out the Lights (and Go to Sleep)," and "Baby's Blue."

Frances Williams was a versatile stage and screen performer best known for her work in the 1930s. Born in St. Paul, Minnesota in 1901, she left home as a teenager and began performing as an acrobat. Her singing and dancing skills brought her to New York, where she appeared on Broadway with the Marx Brothers in *The Cocoanuts*.

When *Everybody's Welcome* closed after 139 performances, "As Time Goes By" was virtually forgotten, except by a Cornell University student named Murray Burnett who bought the recording and played it so often that his fraternity brothers at Pi Lambda Phi got sick of listening to it.

In the summer of 1938, Burnett, then a 27-year-old high school English teacher, made a trip to Europe with his wife. What he saw in Vienna so horrified him that, on his return to New York, he decided to write an anti-Nazi play. After a few false starts, he and writer friend Joan Alison collaborated on *Everybody Comes to Rick's*, a play that included the song "As Time Goes By."

The protagonist in *Everybody Comes to Rick's* is a cynical, unhappily married American expatriate who owns a nightclub in Casablanca. His former lover Lois appears at the club with the Resistance leader, Victor Laszlo, and asks Sam, the club's black piano player, to play "As Time Goes By." Lois' passion for Rick is rekindled. She decides to stay with him in Casablanca. In Victor's presence Rick insists that she leave. Victor, despite having been humiliated by her, takes her with him.

The vast bulk of the plot in *Casablanca* was derived from the original play.

When Irene Lee, Warner studio's West Coast story editor, stopped in to rummage through the piles of manuscripts lining Jack Wilk's New York office, she found only one interesting property – a dog-eared typed manuscript in a dusty three-hole ringbinder – *Everybody Comes to Rick's*. Lee suggested it to Jack Warner, who agreed to buy it for $20,000. The studio's executive in charge of production, Hal B. Wallis, decided to make the film, and changed the title as an attempt to recapture the exotic appeal of the 1938 Hedy Lamarr vehicle *Algiers*.

Harold Brent Wallis, born in Chicago, Illinois, on September 14, 1898, started in the publicity department at Warner Brothers in 1923. By 1928 he had worked his way up to producer, and in 1933 had taken over as chief producer when Darryl Zanuck left to form 20th Century.

In early 1942, Wallis signed a contract that allowed him to leave his job as head of production to run his own company, Hal Wallis Productions. In that year, he made six pictures for Warner Brothers to distribute: *Desperate Journey, Now, Voyager, Watch on the Rhine, Air Force, Princess O'Rourke*, and *Casablanca*. Not a bad year.

Everybody Comes to Rick's was written with a cast of sixteen speaking parts plus extras. Hal Wallis and Michael Curtiz had encouraged the screenwriters to revise the play and write additional scenes, giving *Casablanca* twenty-two speaking roles and hundreds of extras for atmosphere.

The screenplay became a triumph of creativity over committee. Not long after Hal Wallis decided to personally shepherd *Casablanca* from script to screen, Aeneas MacKenzie and Wally Kline spent six weeks working on an adaptation of the original play. Afterwards, Julius and Philip G. Epstein came on board, and worked on the overall structure and dialogue. Howard Koch was instructed to start the screenplay all over again, paying particular attention to Rick's background and the ending, while the Epsteins were still struggling with their version. The three writers seemed to do very little in the way of actual collaboration. Each wrote scenes and presented them to Wallis and Curtiz for approval.

Known in Hollywood as "The Boys," Julius J. Epstein and Philip G. Epstein were lanky identical twins who had earned a reputation in the movie business for adapting plays, doctoring weak scripts, and adding memorable wisecracks and colorful dialogue to clichéd stories. Mediocre scripts for films like *Yankee Doodle Dandy* were energized after the Epsteins got finished with them and went on to become classics.

They had come to Warner Brothers after graduating from Penn State University, where they developed a reputation as writers of snappy dialogue and memorable one-liners, in spite of their love-hate relationship with studio head Jack Warner who deplored their work habits – the boys usually worked only two hours a day.

Julius once explained, "I write only when I absolutely have to. If I wanted to work every day I'd have gone into the dress business."

Screenwriters Philip and Julius Epstein are the grandfather and great-uncle, respectively, of Theo Epstein, the former general manager of the Boston Red Sox who, in 2004, lead them to their first World Series championship in 86 years.

Born in New York City, Howard Koch grew up in Kingston, New York, attended St. Stephen's College (later renamed Bard College) and earned a law degree at Columbia before becoming a writer for the *CBS Mercury Theater of the Air.* He wrote the Orson Welles radio drama *The War of the Worlds,* broadcast on October 30, 1938, which caused nationwide panic among some listeners for its documentary-like portrayal of an invasion of spaceships from Mars. Koch began writing for Hollywood studios, and as a liberal activist he was brought in to strengthen the political and dramatic aspects of the *Casablanca* screenplay.

After the war, Koch was fired by Jack Warner after Koch was denounced as a Communist. He was criticized by the House Un-American Activities Committee for his outspoken leftist political views and blacklisted by Hollywood in 1951.

After graduating from Cornell University at age 19, Casey Robinson briefly taught English before opting for a career in journalism. Through one of his newspaper contacts, he made his entree into films in 1927 as a title writer. He spent most of the 1930s and a portion of the early '40s at Warner Brothers, where he scripted some of the studio's most successful "women's films" (among them *Four Daughters, Dark Victory*, and *Now, Voyager*). With a gift for handling emotionally difficult material, Robinson was brought in to flesh out the romantic entanglement of Rick and Ilsa, although many of his suggestions did not end up in the film. He turned down a screen credit – missing out on an Academy Award – because of his insistence on taking credit only for scripts he wrote entirely by himself.

Rick Blaine's love interest was originally written as an American, and the studio thought that Ann Sheridan (who had already shared billing on six pictures with Bogart) would be perfect in the role. But the leading lady was changed into a European by screenwriter Casey Robinson who at the time was "falling in love with a Russian ballerina named Tamara Toumanova." Robinson even persuaded the studio to test Toumanova for the part.

With black silky hair, deep brown eyes and pale almond skin, Toumanova was called "the loveliest creature in the history of the ballet." In 1966 she played the lead ballerina in Alfred Hitchcock's political thriller *Torn Curtain.*

It was director Michael Curtiz who came up with a new name for the European heroine. His source was the nineteenth century poem, "Journey Through the Harz Mountains" by Heinrich Heine, whose main character is an enchantress named Princess Ilse.

At the 16th Academy Awards, Julius Epstein, Philip Epstein and Howard Koch received the "Best Screenplay" Oscar for their work on the film. (The Epstein brothers became the only pair of twins to ever win an Oscar). And while *Casablanca* would have been the high point of his career, Murray Burnett, co-author of the original play, never received credit for the script and lost multiple lawsuits over the issue.

Another Burnett play, *Hickory Street*, had a short Broadway run in 1944 and he later wrote episodes for the radio spy series, *Cafe Istanbul*, hosted by Marlene Dietrich.

Michael Curtiz began directing films in his native Hungary in 1912. After World War I, he continued his filmmaking career in Austria and Germany and into the early 1920s when he directed films in other countries in Europe. Moving to the US in 1926, he started making films in Hollywood for Warner Brothers and *Casablanca* was one of eight films Michael Curtiz and Humphrey Bogart did together.

When writer Howard Koch protested that some of the scenes were illogical, Curtiz retorted in his fractured English: "Don't worry what's logical. I make it go so fast no one notices." And he did – he relied upon speed of direction to conceal the plot's numerous holes.

The director's use of shadows and high contrast lighting to activate his frame was long-established in his Hollywood career before film noir was labeled a stylistic signature.

In an interview with Peter Bogdanovich, Howard Hawks said that he was supposed to direct *Casablanca* and Michael Curtiz was supposed to direct *Sergeant York*. During conversation over lunch, Hawks said that he didn't know how to make this "musical comedy," while Curtiz replied that he didn't know anything about "those hill people." They switched projects. Hawks explained that he considered *Casablanca* a musical comedy because of the number of singing scenes in the café.

After viewing the completed film, Hawks said, "I liked it, but I never had any faith in my doing anything like that."

Arthur Edeson began his career as a still photographer, but turned to movies in 1911 as a camera operator for the Societe Francaise des Films at Cinematographs Éclair, the French-owned film studio in Fort Lee, New Jersey. In the early thirties, perhaps his most memorable creative partnership was formed with director James Whale, for whom he photographed the first three of Whale's quartet of horror films: *Frankenstein, The Old Dark House*, and *The Invisible Man*.

As cinematographer for *Casablanca*, Arthur Edeson paid particular attention to photographing Bergman. She was shot mainly from her preferred left side, often with a softening gauze filter and with catch lights to make her eyes sparkle; the whole effect was designed to make her face seem "ineffably sad and tender and nostalgic. He used dark film noir and expressionist lighting in several scenes, particularly towards the end of the picture.

His father was an architect and field engineer of the Gotthard Rail Tunnel through the Alps. Carl Jules Weyl studied at the École des Beaux-Arts in Paris before immigrating to America in 1912. He worked as an architect in California, first in San Francisco, then in Los Angeles, where he designed the majority of Hollywood Boulevard's flamboyant Spanish Colonial Revival commercial buildings. His design of the Brown Derby restaurants, shaped like derby hats, was intended to capture the attention of passing motorists.

Weyl joined Warner Brothers, under contract from 1934 to 1947. As the Art Director on *Casablanca*, he accomplishes what is known as "invisible style," a nuanced way of designing where subtle elements like a table filled with champagne coupes, or the whirl of airplane propellers on a foggy runway, end up meaning as much to a narrative as dialogue.

The setting for Rick's Café Américain, designed by Art Director Carl Jules Weyl, was modeled after interiors of the El Minzah in Tangiers, a luxurious hotel built in 1930 by John Crichton-Stuart, a British aristocrat heavily mired in the shady business of the enclave known as the International Zone. The hotel was intended to combine the architectural heritage of Morocco with the comfort of an English gentleman's club. Situated on the Straits of Gibraltar, where Europe and Africa almost touch, the El Minzah was the fashionable heart of "International Tangiers." Guests have included Winston Churchill and Barbara Hutton. Producers recreated the setting for the grand sum of $9,200.

Rick's Cafe was one of the few original sets built for the film, the rest were recycled from other Warner Brothers productions due to wartime restrictions on building supplies. The opening street bazaar scenes were filmed on the backlot built for *The Desert Song*. The Paris train station set was recycled from *Now, Voyager*.

The entire film (except for the opening airport scenes filmed at the Van Nuys municipal airport) was filmed on the Warner Brothers sound stage in Burbank. Even the final airfield scene was shot in the studio, using a wooden airplane veneer and "midgets" to give the runway and its crew the illusion of distance and scale. This visual deception was masked by the abundant fog (although real-life Casablanca is desert-bound and rarely, if ever, has fog).

George Raft, looking to shed his tough-guy image, was angling for the lead role of Rick with Jack Warner, but Hal Wallis had never considered anyone but Humphrey Bogart for its starring role.

Studio publicity in 1941 claimed that Ronald Reagan and Ann Sheridan were scheduled to appear in the film, and Dennis Morgan was mentioned as the third lead. This was never the case, of course, and the false story was planted, either by a studio publicist or a press agent for the three other actors, to keep their names in the press.

The film's opening montage sequence was created by Don Siegel, head of the studio's film library montage department. Siegel went on to direct many films himself, often transcending the limitations of budget and script to produce interesting and adept works. He made the original *Invasion of the Body Snatchers* in 1956. He directed Elvis Presley in *Flaming Star*, Steve McQueen in *Hell Is for Heroes* and Lee Marvin in *The Killers* before directing a series of five films with Clint Eastwood.

He was the staff announcer at KFWB and the voice of Warner previews. In addition, Lou Marcelle had played the good Doctor in *The Shadow of Fu Man-chu*, a popular radio series recorded in Hollywood at Radio Recorders studios in the winter of 1938-39. His dramatic narration at the beginning of *Casablanca* explained the "tortuous refugee trail" that included the Moroccan city as an "embarkation" point to neutral Lisbon. (The narration was notable for his unorthodox pronunciation of visas a "veezays.")

Bogart was given one of the most memorable "entrances" in film history. After scrawling his "OK" across the back of a check, he appears, clad in a white tuxedo jacket and black bowtie, sitting alone at the table, his face devoid of expression.

Rick and Ilsa standing over Sam's piano in Paris was the first scene to be shot. Filming a love scene with two actors who had just met was not planned, but the filming of *Now, Voyager* had gone over schedule, so Paul Henreid and Claude Rains were not yet available.

The phrase, "I'm shocked, shocked!" was borrowed from an early Warner Brothers film, *Five Star Final* (1931), the line spoken by Boris Karloff who plays an unscrupulous tabloid reporter by the name of T. Vernon Isopod. The film was based on a play written by Louis Weitzenkorn after his stint as editor of *The New York Evening Graphic*, a sensationalist tabloid of the 1920s. In 1936, *Five Star Final* was remade as *Two Against the World*, a film that starred Humphrey Bogart – six years before *Casablanca*.

Just before he shoots Major Strasser (Conrad Veidt), Bogart ad-libbed the line, "All right, Major, you asked for it." But Wallis thought it looked as though when Strasser drew his gun first it was self-defense. The scene reshot without the line, but the original version was used in the trailer for the film.

Bogart's line of resignation that he can't escape Ilsa was previously written as, "Of all the cafés in all the towns in the world, she walks into my café. The use of "gin joints" is attributed to Bogart himself.

She has been called the most beautiful woman ever to appear in films, and she was the producer's first choice to play Ilsa. Hal Wallis wanted Hedy Lamarr for the role, but she was under contract to MGM (which wouldn't release her), and she didn't want to work with an unfinished script anyway (she later turned down the female lead in *Gaslight*, another role that went to Ingrid Bergman).

During the heyday of her career, Lamarr and her friend, the composer George Antheil, received a patent for an idea of a radio signaling device, or "Secret Communications System," that later became an important step in the development of technology to maintain the security of both military communications and cellular phones.

The studio tested blond French actress Michèle Morgan for the part of Ilsa. She asked for $55,000, but Wallis refused to pay it when he could get the young, womanly, Swedish beauty Ingrid Bergman for $25,000.

Ingrid Bergman's contract was owned by producer David O. Selznick, and producer Hal B. Wallis sent the film's writers, Philip G. Epstein and Julius J. Epstein, to persuade Selznick to loan her to Warner Brothers for the picture. After 20 minutes of describing the plot to Selznick, Julius gave up and said, "Oh, what the hell! It's a lot of shit like *Algiers*. A lot of cigarette smoke and guitar music." Selznick said, "Okay, you've got Bergman."

According to assistant director Lee Katz, Curtiz called Ingrid Bergman "Christmas Baby" because "she looked like something you'd love to have for Christmas."

Born Swedish immigrants in Cleveland, Ruth Stenius Roberts followed her brother George to Los Angeles. (As George Seaton he became a successful screenwriter, director, and producer). In 1938, when Ingrid Bergman came to Hollywood to star in the English remake of *Intermezzo*, the studio hired Ruth, who had previously trained Hedy Lamarr, to smooth the edges off the rising star's Swedish accent. She continued as Ingrid's dialect coach on *Casablanca*, and the two women became close friends. As for one of the film's most memorable lines – "Here's looking at you, kid" – Bogart picked up the line from Ruth who was simultaneously teaching Ingrid poker and slang one day during a lunch break.

Writer Julius Epstein later said, "What would that line have been without Bogie, coming out of the mouth of some other actor, any other actor? He lives forever saying that line."

He was born on April 3, 1886, in Tyler, Texas. Arthur Wilson broke into show business at the age of 12, appearing in a vaudeville minstrel show. He sang and played the drums in black clubs in the Tyler area before moving to Chicago, where he earned the nickname "Dooley" from his signature performance of the Irish song, "Mr. Dooley." His performance in the Broadway production of *Cabin in the Sky* led to his signing with the Paramount studio in Hollywood.

Hal Wallis thought of changing the role of Sam to a woman, and suggestions included Lena Horne, Ella Fitzgerald, and Hazel Scott. Wilson won the role of Sam over top contender Clarence Muse, a veteran black actor who had just played Bela Lugosi's butler in *The Invisible Ghost*. (Muse later played Sam in a 1950s TV adaptation of *Casablanca*).

Dooley Wilson was a professional drummer who had to fake playing the piano. The piano sequences were recorded live on the set, not prerecorded, and were actually played by pianist Elliot Carpenter just out of camera range. Wilson sang while stealing glimpses of Carpenter's hands in order to make his playing seem authentic. He became skilled at duplicating Carpenter's finger and hand movements in synchronization with the music. (Carpenter received no screen credit).

Besides "As Time Goes By," Wilson's character performs "It Had To Be You," "Shine," "Knock On Wood," and "Arlez-moi D'amour."

Racial equality was not a reality at the time, and although Sam is treated kindly and respectfully at certain parts of the movie, he is belittled for much of the movie as well. Ilsa, on her first visit to Rick's, refers to Sam as "the boy who is playing the piano" although he is at least 10 years her senior. Sam consistently obeys Rick's every order with a "yes, suh," like a slave with a benevolent master.

Trained as a coloratura soprano from a very young age, Corinna Mura learned to play guitar and became a nightclub performer. She went on to star on her own radio program called *The Corinna Mura International Salon*, and she performed in the White House for President Franklin D. Roosevelt on three occasions. She made her mark in *Casablanca* as Andrea, the singer at Rick's Café who plays "Tango Della Rose" while Victor Lazlo goes to the bar to talk to Burger. She is later seen giving a disdainful look to Strasser and the group of Nazis who come into Rick's, then joins in with the singing of "La Marseilles." Upon marrying journalist Edward Lee Gorey, Mura became the stepmother of writer and artist Edward Gorey, noted for his illustrated books.

Trained by the great classical music composers Johannes Brahms and Robert Fuchs, Maximilian Raoul "Max" Steiner was a music prodigy who conducted his first operetta when he was twelve and became a full-time professional, either composing, arranging or conducting, when he was fifteen. He was the first composer to use orchestral music to enhance the effect of films, with *King Kong* and *Gone With the Wind* to his credit before composing the score for *Casablanca*.

Steiner didn't like "As Time Goes By" and suggested his own love theme. But Hal Wallis insisted on keeping the song, and Steiner made it the leitmotif of his score.

The music heard over the film's opening credits was originally written and used the theme for the 1934 John Ford film, *The Lost Patrol*. Steiner slightly altered the tempo and instrumentation of this theme music for *Casablanca*.

W hile in high school, M. K. Jerome was a vaudeville pianist and accompanist in movie theaters, then became a staff pianist for sheet music publishers Waterson, Berlin and Snyder. He came to Hollywood in 1929, and wrote theme songs for early film musicals, under contract to Warner Brothers for eighteen years. Jack Scholl got his start penning lyrics in conjunction with such tunesmiths as Eubie Blake.

Although M.K. Jerome and Jack Scholl are listed in the opening credits for "Songs," they are in fact represented by only one song, "Knock on Wood." The other song they wrote for *Casablanca*, "Dat's What Noah Done," was cut from the picture.

A song of love and betrayal, "Perfidia" was written by Alberto Domínguez, a Mexican composer and arranger, born in the state of Chiapas. The tune is played in the flashback sequence when Ilsa and Rick dance in the Paris nightclub. (Argentine-born actor Barry Norton, an extra in the film, worked with Bogart on his dance steps). Aside from the original Spanish, other renditions exist, including English and instrumental versions. The English lyrics are by Milton Leeds. The song was published in 1939 and became a hit for Xavier Cugat in 1940.

During the shoot, Bogart was called to the studio to stand in the middle of the Rick's Cafe set and nod silently. He had no idea what the nod meant in the story – that he was giving his okay for the band in the cafe to play "La Marseillaise." (The scene was inspired by Jean Renoir's 1937 film, *Grand Illusion*, in which French service members in a German POW camp sing the song as a similar gesture of defiance). The power in this scene stems from the emotional values of the songs as they represent the two strongly opposed forces in war.

As Rick gives the band permission to play the French national anthem, Victor Laszlo leads patrons in belting out the song. Their voices drown out Major Strasser's troops singing "Die Wacht am Rhein," a symbolic political and emotional victory, captured in the close-up of impassioned Yvonne and her poignant battle cry.

Vive La France! With that declaration and her tear-streaked face, French actress Madeleine LeBeau turns the small but crucial role of Yvonne into one of film's indelible moments.

In the scene where "La Marseillaise" is sung over "Die Wacht Am Rhein," many of the extras had real tears in their eyes, a large number of them actual refugees from Nazi persecution in Germany, overcome by the emotions of the scene.

In fact, the Warner Brothers studio commissary at lunch, with its mix of nationalities and accents, may not have been all that different from Rick's Café. The influx into Hollywood of large numbers of European exiles fleeing the war helped the casting enormously. In fact, of all the featured players in the film who get screen credit, only three were born in the United States: Humphrey Bogart, Dooley Wilson and Joy Page.

Warner Brothers claimed that people of 34 nationalities worked on the film .

Producer Wallis had intended to use "Horst-Wessel-Lied," the anthem of the Nazi party, sung by the German SS soldiers during the anthem standoff sequence, but the copyright was controlled by a German company, and the studio dropped that anthem for the lesser "Die Wacht Am Rhein" rather than violate the rights (which would have prompted the German copyright holder on the song to prohibit the movie from being shown in any country not at war with Germany).

"Bright College Years" is one of the traditional songs of Yale University, written to the tune of "Die Wacht am Rhein" in 1881 by Henry Strong Durand. The song has been the unofficial alma mater that, with handkerchief accompaniment, is a standard element of commencement, football games, and alumni get-togethers.

When Rick and Ilsa are listening to the sound of German guns out the window in Paris, Rick comments that they are from the "New German 77s." Actually, the German Army used a 77-mm field gun in World War I, not World War II.

German companies Krupp and Erhardt designed and built the Model 77-mm to compete in the field against the French 75-mm, according to William C. Dooly Jr., in his book, *Great Weapons of World War I.*

Captain Renault says, "We mustn't underestimate American blundering. I was with them when they blundered into Berlin in 1918." This is clearly an historical overstatement by Renault. The American Expeditionary Force fought on the Western Front during the Aisne Offensive (at Château-Thierry and Belleau Wood) in June 1918, and fought its major actions in the Saint-Mihiel and Meuse-Argonne Offensives in late 1918. Late in the war American units ultimately fought in two other theaters at the request of European powers; Pershing sent troops of the 332nd Infantry to Italy, and President Wilson agreed to send troops, the 27th and 339th Infantry Regiments, to Russia.

In Europe, under the name of Fritz van Dongen, Philip Dorn made films from the time that he was fourteen. In Hollywood from 1939, he often played anti-Nazi patriots and continental lovers. It was rumored that he would be joining the cast of the upcoming *Casablanca*, playing the role of Victor Laszlo. Besides Dorn, Herbert Marshall, Dean Jagger and Joseph Cotten were considered for the role, until Paul Henreid became available.

Paul Henreid was born on January 10, 1908, in Trieste, then a part of Austria. His full name was Paul George Julius von Hernreid, the son a prominent Viennese banker. He studied drama in Vienna before fleeing Hitler's Europe, and like the fictional Victor Lazlo, he was a staunchly anti-Nazi.

Henreid was loaned to Warners for the role of Victor Lazlo by Selznick International Pictures against his will. He was concerned that playing a secondary character would ruin his career as a romantic lead, but it was his friend (and co-star in *Now, Voyager*), Bette Davis, who convinced him that he could make the character interesting. Henreid (along with Ingrid Bergman) makes his first appearance 24 minutes into the film.

In *Now, Voyager*, Henreid and Bette Davis created one of the screen's most imitated scenes, in which he lights two cigarettes and hands one to her.

The son of Romanian-Jewish immigrant parents, Marcel Dalio performed in stage plays in the 1920s and had major roles in two of Jean Renoir's most famous films, *Grand Illusion* and *The Rules of the Game*. After divorcing his first wife, he married seventeen-year-old actress Madeleine LeBeau in 1938. In June 1940, LeBeau and Dalio left Paris ahead of the invading German army.

In 1942, he appeared as Emil the croupier in *Casablanca* (for which he was paid $667). In one of the film's memorable scenes, when Renault closes down Rick's Café Americain using the pretext, "I am shocked, shocked to find that gambling is going on in here," Emil approaches, hands him money and says, "Your winnings, sir."

His wife Madeleine LeBeau played Yvonne, Rick's on-again, off-again girlfriend. She had earlier roles in *Hold Back the Dawn* and *Gentleman Jim*. Before *Casablanca* finished shooting, Dalio filed for divorce on grounds of his wife's desertion.

Hustled out of the café by Rick, Yvonne returns the next night on the arm of a German Officer (Hans Twardowski) and is mocked by a French Officer (Alberto Morin) for crawling in to bed with the enemy. In real life, Twardowski had left Germany because he was a homosexual, a group targeted for persecution by the Nazis. A close friend of Marlene Dietrich, he appeared with her in 1934's *The Scarlet Empress*.

Born in Puerto Rico and educated in France, Alberto Morin worked briefly for Pathé Freres, then signed with Fox Pictures to make Spanish-language films for the South American market. He remained in Hollywood as a character actor, playing René Picard (Maybelle Merriwether's beau) in *Gone with the Wind* before his uncredited role in *Casablanca*.

Curt Bois was born in Berlin and began acting in 1907, becoming one of the film world's first child actors. His career spanned eighty years, a longer period than can be claimed by any other actor. In 1934, Bois was forced to leave his home for America, where he found work on stage on Broadway. By 1937, he had made his way to Hollywood, and began acting in American films, best-known for his portrayal of the pickpocket in *Casablanca*, warning a couple about "vultures, vultures everywhere," then leaving with the man's wallet.

After World War II, Bois decided it was safe to return to Germany, where in 1987 he played Homer, the aged poet in Wim Wenders' German-language romantic fantasy film, *Wings of Desire*.

Born as Guillermo Bocconcini in Italy, he immigrated to the United States and began acting under the name William Edmunds, typically playing roles with heavy accents. He has a brief appearance in *Casablanca* where in Rick's Café he gives instructions to a man seeking illegal passage out of Casablanca. His most notable role was Giuseppe Martini, the Italian bar owner in *It's a Wonderful Life*.

After Hitler's forces took over Austria in 1938, Lutz Altschul came to America and changed his name to Louis V. Arco. He received one scene as a refugee in *Casablanca*, seen in the introduction to Rick's Café looking very depressed. He has one line, "waiting, waiting, waiting.... I'll never get out of here.... I'll die in Casablanca." Arco died at age 75, not in Casablanca, as his character says in the movie, but in Zürich, Switzerland.

Born to a Russian Jewish family in Montréal, Québec, Canada, George London grew up in Los Angeles. A bass-baritone with a large, resonant voice, he appears in *Casablanca* in a French Foreign Legion uniform singing "La Marseillaise."

After performing widely with tenor Mario Lanza and soprano Frances Yeend as part of the Bel Canto Trio in 1947 and 1948, London was engaged by the Vienna State Opera, where he scored his first major success in 1949.

Abdul the Arab, who guarded the door at Rick's Café, was portrayed by character actor Dan Seymour. A native of Chicago, Seymour began his career as a song and dance comic in burlesque theater and nightclubs in New York. But when he moved to Hollywood, the burly 250-pound actor was cast as a villain, the character he played in most of his 70 films and 300 television roles.

In addition to *Casablanca*, Seymour appeared in other Bogart films, including *To Have and Have Not* in 1944 and *Key Largo* in 1948. He played the chief of police in the Marx Brothers spoof, *A Night in Casablanca*.

B orn in Odessa, Ukraine, Leon Belasco was prepared for a musical career at various seats of learning in Japan and Manchuria. For several years, he was first violinist for the Tokyo Symphony, and later led his own orchestra. Prior to acting, Belasco was leader of a society orchestra which had the distinction of introducing the Andrews Sisters to American audiences. (They went on to become the most popular female vocal group of the first half of the 20th century).

He enjoyed a 60-year career in film and television from the 1920s to the 1980s. In 1942, Belasco appeared in 13 different films, including *Holiday Inn, Yankee Doodle Dandy, Road to Morocco*, and *Casablanca* in the role of a dealer in Rick's Café.

A reliable British stage, screen, and radio actor, Gerald Oliver Smith came to Hollywood in 1937 and played scores of bit parts, often proper English gentlemen complete with monocle and haughty demeanor. Smith played the pickpocketed Englishman in *Casablanca*.

Born in London, the daughter of a retired sea captain, Norma Varden was a child prodigy. She trained as a concert pianist in Paris and performed in England before deciding to take up acting. She began to appear in British films, usually in haughty upper class roles. Visiting California with her ailing mother in the 1940s, she decided to settle permanently, beginning her American film career as the wife of the pickpocketed Englishman in *Casablanca*. Among her later roles, she played the housekeeper Frau Schmidt in *The Sound of Music*.

Leonid Kinskey was born in St. Petersburg, Russia. He fled the Russian Revolution and performed across Europe and in South America before he arrived in the United States in the 1930s. His first film role was in Ernst Lubitsch's 1932 comedy *Trouble in Paradise*. A year later he appeared with the Marx Brothers in *Duck Soup*. It is said that he got the role of Sascha, the bartender in *Casablanca*, because he was a drinking buddy of Humphrey Bogart.

In a memorable scene, Bogart as Rick arranges for a young Hungarian couple, played by Helmut Dantine and Joy Page, to win enough at roulette to pay for an exit visa, which spares the beautiful young wife the need to obtain the document by sleeping with the chief of police, portrayed by Claude Rains. Sascha, overcome by the usually cynical Rick's romantic generosity, kisses him and says, "Boss, you've done a beautiful thing." And Rick snarls, "Go away, you crazy Russian."

Jan Brandel believes that the only hope of escaping Casablanca is by winning big at the roulette table. The character is played by Helmut Dantine who was born in Vienna in 1917, the son of head of the Austrian railway system. As a young man, Dantine became involved in an anti-Nazi movement, and was imprisoned when the Nazis took over Austria. Three months later, using their influence, his parents obtained his release and sent him to California, where he began an acting career at the Pasadena Playhouse. Dantine spent the early 1940s at Warner Brothers, and after appearing in *Casablanca*, he received his first lead role in *Edge of Darkness* in 1943.

B orn in Germany, he grew up in England where he started his stage career. In 1915, Leo White began appearing in Charlie Chaplin's comedies, including a small role in *The Great Dictator*, released in 1940. He often played dapper, continental villains or noblemen in films. In *Casablanca* he appears as waiter Emile (not to be confused with the croupier Emil), from whom Renault orders a drink when he sits down with Ilsa and Laszlo.

Joy Page played Jan Brandel's young Bulgarian wife who faces having to sleep with the corrupt police captain played by Claude Rains to obtain exit visas to escape from Casablanca. Born Joy Cerrette Paige on November 9, 1924, in Los Angeles, she was the daughter of the silent-film star Don Alvarado and Ann Boyar, who married Jack L. Warner, head of the Warner Brothers studio, after she and Mr. Alvarado divorced. Warner did not encourage his seventeen-year-old stepdaughter's interest in acting. She read for the part and landed the role on her own, and although Warner reluctantly approved, he refused to sign her to a studio contract or cast her in other Warner Brothers films.

Born in Lockenhaus, Austria, Ludwig Stössel was one of many Jewish actors and actresses who were forced to flee Europe when the Nazis came to power in 1933. A few months after coming to America, at the age of 59, he received the role of Mr. Leuchtag, who along with his wife are leaving Europe for America in Casablanca. Having a brandy in Rick's Café with Carl the waiter and struggling a bit with their English, he asks his wife (Ilka Grünig) for the time, "Liebchen, sweetnessheart, what watch?" She answers, "Ten watch" and he replies "such much." Carl assures them they will get along beautifully in America. (The German translation for 10 o'clock is zehn Uhr, however Uhr is also the German word for clock or in this case watch, thus ten watch).

Stössel appeared in supporting roles in over 40 movies after *Casablanca*, including another Humphrey Bogart film, *Action in the North Atlantic.*

At the age of 66, she was the oldest actor in *Casablanca*. Ilka Grüning received the role of Mrs. Leuchtag, who along with her husband (played by Ludwig Stössel) are leaving Europe for America. She has only one scene (a total of 30 words) in the movie when she and her husband are having a drink in Rick's Cafe with their good friend Carl the waiter (S.Z. Sakall) and struggling a bit with their English.

Born in Sicily, Frank Puglia began his career as a teen on stage in Italian operas. He emigrated to America in 1907 and worked in a laundry before joining an Italian-language theater group in New York. While appearing on stage, he was discovered by D. W. Griffith, which began an acting career spanning over 150 films. In *Casablanca*, he plays the Morroccan merchant who marks down prices to friends of Rick.

Originally cast as Bonasera the undertaker in Francis Ford Coppola's *The Godfather*, illness forced Puglia to withdraw from the role shortly before shooting began.

Torben Emil Meyer was born in Copenhagen, Denmark and began his career as a stage actor in Denmark. He arrived in Hollywood just when the transition to sound was in progress, and in contrast to many other European-born actors, his thick accent became an asset for him. He played the Dutch banker in *Casablanca* who is seated at a baccarat table. His female friend (played by Trude Berliner) wants to have a drink with Rick but is told no by Carl, the headwaiter. Meyer is annoyed by this rebuff telling Carl, "Perhaps if you told him I ran the second largest banking house in Amsterdam." He is informed that it wouldn't impress Rick, "the leading banker in Amsterdam is now the pastry chef in our kitchen" and "his father is the bell-boy!"

Trude Berliner, the woman at the baccarat table who asks if Rick will have a drink with her, was a well-known cabaret performer who left Germany when Hitler and the Nazi Party came to power in 1933 and immigrated to the United States. Carl responds, "Madame, he never drinks with customers. Never. I have never seen it."

Playing the Dutch banker's wife in *Casablanca* was her first part in an American movie. She had another bit part in MGM's *Reunion in France* starring John Wayne and Joan Crawford. (Young Ava Gardner had a small role in the same film).

Brooklyn-born George Meeker switched from stage to screen in the silent era, playing leading roles in such features as *Four Sons* (1928). In talkies, he was frequently cast as a caddish "other man," the guy you loved to hate. In *Casablanca*, Meeker shows up as the white-suited gent who turns to Bogart after the arrest of Ugarte and sneers, "When they come to get me, Rick, I hope you'll be more of a help." (An expert polo player, Meeker was just as much in demand for his skills on the polo field as he was in films).

A typo in the credits lists veteran character actor S.Z. Sakall as "S.K. Sakall." Hungarian-born, chubby-jowled Sakall played numerous supporting roles in Hollywood musicals and comedies in the 1940s and 1950s. He looked like a dumpling, earned the nickname "Cuddles," and became famous for using the phrase "everything is hunky dunky." His first big hit was *Ball of Fire* with Gary Cooper and Barbara Stanwyck. At the age of 59, he portrayed his most famous character, Carl the head waiter in *Casablanca*, for which he received $5,250. (He actually had more screen time than either Peter Lorre or Sydney Greenstreet).

British actor Herbert Evans played countless butlers, bobbies, store clerks, porters and pursers. In *Casablanca*, his character questions the casino's honesty: "Say, are you sure this place is honest?" Sakall (as Carl) replies, "Honest! As honest as the day is long!"

Wolfgang Zilzer was born in Cincinnati, Ohio to German-Jewish emigrant Max Zilzer, who was engaged at the local theater. Zilzer's mother died soon after his birth and his father returned to Germany in 1905. He returned to the United States to work with Ernst Lubitsch in several anti-Nazi movies, using pseudonyms to protect his father, who was still living in Berlin. In *Casablanca*, he was cast as the "man with expired papers."

Zilzer was married to Lotte Palfi who played the woman selling her diamonds in the film. She was an aspiring Jewish stage actress who fled Germany in 1934 with her first husband, film editor Victor Palfi, after the Nazis came to power. In the 1976 film, *Marathon Man*, she played "the woman on 47th street," chasing a Nazi who is trying to escape with robbed diamonds.

The couple divorced in old age when Zizler wanted to die in Germany and his wife refused to return to her native country.

Agraduate of Columbia University and a veteran stage actor, New York-born Charles La Torre played the Italian military officer Tonelli, an officer who strives unsuccessfully to catch Major Strasser's attention and comes across as hapless and buffoonish. Later, when Tolelli is arguing with a subordinate of Renault, Renault notes that if Tonelli "gets a word in edgewise it will be a major Italian victory."

Born in St. Petersburg, Russia, Gregory Gaye was a cadet in the Russian navy and began his stage career in Europe and in the Orient before coming to the United States after the Russian Revolution in 1917. He appeared in small roles in over a hundred films, but most notably in *Casablanca* as the official of Hitler's Reichsbank who tries to gain entrance to the back-room casino, but is stopped by Abdul (Dan Seymour).

He tells Rick, "I have been in every gambling room between Honolulu and Berlin, and if you think I'm going to be kept out of a saloon like this, you're very much mistaken." Rick tells him, "Your cash is good at the bar." He responds, "What? Do you know who I am?" To which Rick replies, "I do, you're lucky the bar is open to you." Gaye angrily responds, "This is outrageous! I shall report it to *Der Angrif*" (Joseph Goebbels' Nazi newspaper) and storms away.

In what has to be one of the strangest cameos in film history, Rafael Trujillo appears in the background of the airport tarmac in the final scene of *Casablanca*.

Trujillo occupied the Presidency of the Dominican Republic from 1930 until 1938 and again from 1942 until 1952, but always holding absolute power over all Dominican territory. His tyranny, historically known as "La Era de Trujillo" or "The Trujillo Era," is considered one of the bloodiest of the 20th century.

The Chicago Daily News reported that comedian Jack Benny visited the *Casablanca* set at the time Michael Curtiz was directing a café scene featuring Ingrid Bergman and Humphrey Bogart: "There were about 50 extras seated at the small tables and a number of waiters scurrying about. That's where you see Benny, among the waiters. He borrowed a white coat from one of them and appears in the background all during the scene."

John Qualen was born in Vancouver, British Columbia on December 8, 1899, the son of immigrants from Norway. His acting career began at Northwestern University, which he attended on a scholarship won at an oratory contest. Eventually making it to Broadway, he got his big break as the Swedish janitor in Elmer Rice's *Street Scene*, recreating the role in the film version.

Qualen recounted the destruction of his farm by the bank in Ford's *The Grapes of Wrath*, and portrayed confused killer Earl Williams in Howard Hawks' classic comedy *His Girl Friday* before his role as Berger, the jewelry-selling Norwegian Resistance member in *Casablanca*.

French character actor Jean Del Val was a regular in American films beginning in the early days of the talkies. He played the French aviator in *Block-Heads* who rescues over-aged doughboy Stan Laurel from the trenches ("Why, you blockhead. Ze war's been over for twenty years!"), as well as a French Foreign Legion sergeant in *The Flying Deuces*, another Laurel and Hardy comedy. He is the French radio announcer who opens *Casablanca* by spreading the news of the murder of two German couriers carrying letters of transit.

Peter Lorre was born as László Löwenstein in Rózsahegy, Hungary. He began acting on stage in Vienna at the age of 17, then moved to Berlin where he worked with German playwright Bertolt Brecht. Appearing as the child killer in Fritz Lang's *M*, he was noticed by Alfred Hitchcock who cast him in the 1934 version of *The Man Who Knew Too Much*. In the pivotal role of Guillermo Ugarte, the sleazy little black market criminal, Peter Lorre appears for a total of eight minutes in only two scenes, yet *Casablanca* remains one of his best-remembered films. Ugarte is dispatched according to Lorre's preferred mode of exit – screaming in disbelief.

In the film, the spinning of the roulette wheel in Rick's Café symbolized a refugee's chances of securing exit visas. For the cast members, it meant recreation. Peter Lorre claimed that his gambling winnings totaled more than his paycheck.

Sydney Hughes Greenstreet was born in Sandwich, Kent, England, the son of a leather merchant. He left home at age 18 to make his fortune as a Ceylon tea planter, but drought forced him out of business and back to England. He managed a brewery and, to escape boredom, took acting lessons. He toured England with Ben Greet's Shakespearean Company, and in 1905, he made his way to the New York stage. In 1941, Greenstreet made his debut film role as Kasper Gutman ("The Fat Man") in *The Maltese Falcon.*

For his portrayal of Signor Ferrari, owner of the Blue Parrot, Greenstreet wanted to wear something ethnic to show that his character had assimilated into the Moroccan lifestyle. The idea was rejected by producer Hal Wallis who insisted that he wear his now-iconic white suit.

No movie Nazi was more memorable than Conrad Veidt's Major Strasser, the stereotypical villain, ruthlessly cruel and robotically efficient, sent to Casablanca to capture Laszlo.

He was born Hans Walter Conrad Weidt in a working-class district of Berlin, well known in the theatrical community in Germany for his hatred of the Nazis, and forced to hurriedly escape the country when he found out that the SS had sent a death squad after him because of his anti-Nazi activities. After escaping Germany, Veidt settled into a Hollywood career doing his best to portray the Nazis in the worst possible light.

Veidt, whose performance as Strasser was completely different from his own character, died in April 1944, one month after *Casablanca* swept the Academy Awards.

Hungarian-born Richard Ryen began working in Germany as an actor and later became a well-respected stage director at the Munich Chamber Theater. In Hollywood, as was the fate for so many German actors and actresses of that time, he was mainly cast in Nazi roles, which kept him working during the war years.

At age 56, Ryen obtained the role which resulted in his most renowned performance, that of Colonel Heinze in *Casablanca*, where he constantly had to tail his superior Major Heinrich Strasser (Conrad Veidt). He was omitted from the credits.

The son of English stage and film actor Frederick William Rains, young Claude Rains made his debut on the London stage at age eleven and appeared on Broadway in the 1920s. His career spanned 66 years, and while his roles included *The Invisible Man*, a corrupt senator in *Mr. Smith Goes to Washington*, and Mr. Dryden in *Lawrence of Arabia*, none would be as memorable as Captain Renault, the urbane and amoral police chief in *Casablanca* who is always rounding up the usual suspects – and has many of the best lines in the film.

The screenwriters hint that Renault has repressed homosexual feelings for Rick. In one exchange, Renault describes Rick to Ilsa as "the kind of man that, well, if I were a woman and I were not around, I should be in love with Rick." Much has been made over the years about womanizing being a cover for men who resist their true sexual orientation – Renault fits the bill on this accord.

After Strasser is shot, long looks between Rick and Renault cause Renault to tell the police to "round up the usual suspects." He has decided to become a patriot, but perhaps Renault, as a man guided by personal interests, sees this as an opportunity to spend some serious quality time with Rick.

Humphrey Bogart's wife, the eccentric actress Mayo Methot, was pathologically jealous of her husband and routinely threatened violence if he even befriended a female co-star. She continually accused him of having an affair with Ingrid Bergman, often confronting him in his dressing room. Bogart would come onto the set in a rage. In fact, despite the on-screen chemistry between Bogart and Bergman, they hardly spoke at all.

Bergman later explained, "I kissed him, but I never really knew him. He came out of his dressing room, did his scene, then fled away again. It was all very strange and distant."

Bogart was an inch or so shorter than Bergman, so he had to wear lifts in his shoes in their scenes together. Curtiz had Bogart sit on pillows for seated sequences, or had Bergman slouch down (as evident when she sits on the couch in the "franc for your thoughts" scene).

The final script for the film was not completed until after shooting had begun, and Ingrid Bergman did not know until near the end of shooting who her character was really supposed to be in love with, Laszlo or Rick. When she asked director Michael Curtiz to explain, she was told to "play it in between."

The writers pondered having Rick leave with Ilsa, but this was always rejected (and the censors would never have allowed it with her married to Victor). Their major problem was to make it plausible that despite clearly loving Rick she would leave with Victor; the final scene was rewritten many times until this was achieved. After Howard Koch's preferred "sacrifice ending" was shot – Ilsa's escape with Victor – it was mutually decided that it worked so well, the idea of shooting an alternate version was scrapped.

Ingrid Bergman's line, "Victor Laszlo is my husband, and was, even when I knew you in Paris," was almost cut from the film because during that time it was deemed inappropriate for a film to depict or suggest a woman romancing with another man if she were already married. However, it was pointed out that later in the film she explains that she had thought Laszlo was dead at the time, and the censors allowed the line to stay in.

Bergman called the camera her "friend." She considered her left side as her better side, and to the extent possible that was the side photographed throughout the film, so she is almost always on the right side of the screen looking towards the left regardless of who is in the shot with her. The closeups of Bergman, lit by cameraman Arthur Edeson (who also shot *The Maltese Falcon*), are uniformly ravishing. For the scene in which she attempts to extract the letters of transit from Bogart so that she and Henreid may leave Casablanca, Edeson kept his camera almost entirely on her.

Bogart said, "I didn't do anything [in *Casablanca*] I've never done before, but when the camera moves in on that Bergman face, and she's saying she loves you, it would make anybody feel romantic."

A chessboard is part of the introduction to Rick Blaine. The solitary chess game Rick is playing when the camera first focuses on him was an actual game Bogart was playing by mail with a partner in Brooklyn by the name of Irving Kovner, the brother of a studio employee. It was Howard Koch's idea to incorporate the game into the film, explaining it as a metaphor for the Rick-Renault relationship and the "chess-like intrigue which characterizes *Casablanca*."

With script changes nearly every day, Bogart also found time to play chess against Paul Henreid, who said later, "I beat the hell out of him time and time again.

The letters of transit everyone needs to get out of Casablanca are a kind of Hitchcockian MacGuffin. Everybody wants them, but nobody knows quite what they are, only that they are highly desirable. Nazis may not have been squeamish when it came to killing Jews, but try to get them to rip up a couple of letters of transit at the border and apparently they develop ethics. In fact, letters of transit did not exist in Vichy-controlled France — they were merely a plot device invented by the playwrights. Joan Alison said she always expected somebody to challenge her about the letters, but nobody ever did.

A stickler for details, producer Hal Wallis insisted on a real parrot in the Blue Parrot Bar, which, incidentally, became the name of a bar in Manhattan.

Heavy smoking and drinking were common in *Casablanca*-era America. Characters in the film are seen smoking 31 different times, a habit similarly shared by Americans during this period; there was a 14.3 % increase from 1942 to 1943 in the amount of cigarettes manufactured. Americans also mirrored the heavy drinking portrayed in the movie; there was a 50 million gallon increase in alcohol consumption from before the war to 1942.

Early in the film, a man with an expired passport is shot as he attempts to escape from the gendarmes. He falls dead under a wall poster of Marshall Philipp Pétain, clutching a Free France resistance handbill. (The poster includes a quote attributed to Pétain; in English, the quote reads, "I keep my promises, even those of other people.") The lightning defeat of the French army by the Germans in June 1940 had brought down the democratic Third Republic, which was replaced by a French state, headed by Pétain, whose "Vichy regime" collaborated with the Germans. Near the end of the film, when Captain Renault drops the bottle of Vichy water in to the trash, he's symbolically rejecting the German-controlled Vichy government of France.

At the film's end, as Louis and Rick walk side by side down the airport's empty runway, we see that their fates are linked, most overtly in their shared decision to leave Casablanca for Brazzaville, in French Congo. During the war, Brazzaville functioned as the symbolic capital of Free France.

In its use of diffuse light and fog in the cinematic airport scene, its fondness for saloons with their ubiquitous cigarette smoke, and its fascination with morally complex characters, *Casablanca* anticipated the emergence of film noir in the United States, a stylistic movement that has roots in German Expressionist cinematography.

Warner Brothers was the first Hollywood studio to be open about its opposition to the Nazi regime, and the first to prohibit its films from being distributed in Nazi-occupied territories. *Confessions of a Nazi Spy*, released in 1939, was the first blatantly anti-Nazi film produced by a major Hollywood studio prior to World War II. The film stars Edward G. Robinson, Francis Lederer, George Sanders, and a cast of German actors, including some who had emigrated from their country after the rise of Adolf Hitler. Although deliberately propagandistic, it was based on the articles of former FBI agent Leon G. Turrou, who had been active in investigating Nazi spy rings in the United States prior to the war.

There has been persistent confusion as to when *Casablanca* was actually released. The film premiered in New York City on November 26, 1942, in what was called a pre-release engagement. This showing was rushed to theaters to capitalize on the recent events in North Africa, specifically the invasion of American troops into the real Casablanca. Because this kind of free publicity happens only once in a blue moon, the studio rushed *Casablanca* to a theater in New York, but it was not seen by the rest of the country until early 1943, including Los Angeles.

During the height of World War II, *Casablanca* reinforced the prevalent ideas of sacrifice, isolation, intervention and the threat of fascism that inundated American society and the media. The propaganda techniques utilized throughout the film seem intended to reassure American audiences that entering the war in Europe was a good idea and the right thing to do.

President Franklin Roosevelt had watched the newly-released *Casablanca* in the White House residence prior to attending the Casablanca Conference, held at the Anfa Hotel from January 14 to 24, 1943. Roosevelt was joined by British Prime Minister Winston Churchill, and representing the Free French forces, Generals Charles de Gaulle, and Henri Giraud. Premier Joseph Stalin had declined to attend, citing the ongoing conflict in Stalingrad which required his presence in the Soviet Union. The conference produced a unified statement of purpose, the "Casablanca Declaration," which announced to the world that the Allies would accept nothing less than the "unconditional surrender" of the Axis powers.

The Screen Guild Theater was a CBS radio anthology series, broadcast from 1939 until 1952, with leading Hollywood actors performing in adaptations of popular motion pictures. Actors' fees were donated to the Motion Picture Relief Fund, in order to support the creation and maintenance of the Motion Picture Country Home for retired actors. Humphrey Bogart, Ingrid Bergman and Paul Henreid reprised their roles in a Screen Guild performance of *Casablanca* on April 26, 1943.

The film's success led to plans for a sequel, which was to be called *Brazzaville*. Ingrid Bergman was not available, so Geraldine Fitzgerald was considered for the role of Ilsa before the project was (thankfully) killed.

When *Casablanca* won the Academy Award for Best Picture, Jack L. Warner was first on stage to accept the award, beating the film's producer, Hal Wallis, who was incensed at this slight and never forgave Warner.

Wallis left Warner Brothers shortly afterwards to work as an independent producer, enjoying considerable success both commercially and critically. The first screenwriters he hired for his new enterprise were Ayn Rand and Lillian Hellman. Among his financial hits were the Dean Martin and Jerry Lewis comedies and several Elvis Presley movies. He produced *True Grit*, for which John Wayne won the Academy Award for Best Actor of 1969.

The movie's very last line was almost, "Louie, I might have known you'd mix your patriotism with a little larceny." Hal Wallis, intent on ending with a better punch line, came up with his own line after shooting had already been completed. He had to bring Humphrey Bogart back into the studio a month later to dub the new line.

As Rick and Captain Renault are seen from behind, slowly walking across the runway, where the plane carrying Laszlo and Ilsa has just left into the darkness and enveloping fog, Rick says: "Louie, I think this is the beginning of a beautiful friendship." Case closed.

REFERENCES

Sperber, A.M. and Lax, Eric *Bogart* (William Morrow, 1997)

Goldmann, A. J. "Hollywood's German Influence," Wall Street Journal, March 4, 2013.

Prendergast, Roy M. *Film Music: A Neglected Art.* New York: Norton, 1992.

Meyers, Jeffrey. "Bogart and Hemingway," *Virginia Quarterly Review*, Summer, 1996.

Denby, David. "Everybody Comes to Rick's: Casablanca on the Big Screen," *The New Yorker*, March 19, 2012

Spoto, Donald. *Notorious: The Life of Ingrid Bergman* (HarperCollins, 1997).

Chandler, Charlotte. *Ingrid Bergman: A Personal Biography* (Simon & Schuster, 2007).

Youngkin, Stephen D. *The Lost One: A Life of Peter Lorre* (The University Press of Kentucky, 2005)

Harmetz, Aljean Harmetz. *Round Up the Usual Suspects: The Making of Casablanca* (Hyperion, 1992)

Bogdanovich, Peter. *Who the Devil Made It: Conversations with Legendary Film Directors* (Ballantine, 1998)

Robertson, James C. *The Casablanca Man: The Cinema of Michael Curtiz* (Routledge, 1993)

Gianos, Phillip L. *Politics and Politicians in American Film* (Praeger Pulishers, 1998)

Pontuso, James F. *Political Philosophy Comes to Rick's: Casablanca and American Civic Culture* (Lexington Books, 2005)

McCarty, Clifford, *Bogey: The Films of Humphrey Bogart* (Citadel Press, 1965)

Michael, Paul, *Humphrey Bogart: The Man and His Films* (Bonanza Books, 1965)

Warner, Jack, *My First 100 Years in Hollywood* (Random House, 1965)

Quirk, Lawrence J., *The Films of Ingrid Bergman* (Cadillac Publishing, 1971)

Barbour, Alan G., *Humphrey Bogart* (Pyramid Publications, 1973)

Brown, Curtis F., *Ingrid Bergman* (Galahad Books, 1974)

Canham, Kingsley, *The Hollywood Professionals: Michael Curtiz, Raoul Walsh, Henry Hathaway* (Tantivy, 1980)

Walsh, Andrea, *Women's Film and Female Experience, 1940-1950* (Praeger, 1986)

Francisco, Charles, *You Must Remember This: The Filming of "Casablanca,"* (Prentice-Hall, 1980)

Pettigrew, Terence, *Bogart: A Definitive Study of His Film Career* (Proteus Press, 1981)

Rosenzweig, Sidney, *Casablanca and Other Major Films of Michael Curtiz* (UMI Research Press, 1982)

Taylor, John Russell, *Ingrid Bergman* (St. Martin's Press, 1986)

Ray, Robert B., *A Certain Tendency of the Hollywood Cinema 1930-1980* (Princeton University Press, 1985)

Kinnard, Roy, and R.J. Vitone, *The American Films of Michael Curtiz* (Scarecrow Press, 1986)

Leamer, Laurence, *As Time Goes By: The Life of Ingrid Bergman* (Harper-Collins, 1986)

Fuchs, Wolfgang J., *Humphrey Bogart: Cult-Star: A Documentation* (Taco, 1987)

Jarvie, Ian, *Philosophy of the Film* (Routledge, 1987)

Lebo, Harlan, *Casablanca: Behind the Scenes* (Touchstone, 1992)

McArthur, Colin, *The Casablanca File* (John Libbey Cinema and Animation, 1992)

Miller, Frank, *Casablanca: As Time Goes By, 50th Anniversary Commemorative* (Andrews-McMeel Publishing, 1992)

Siegel, Jeff, *The Casablanca Companion: The Movie and More* (Taylor Publishing, 1992)

Osborne, Richard E., *The Casablanca Companion: The Movie Classic and Its Place in History* (Riebel-Roque Publishing Company, 1997)

Whitlock, Cathy, *Designs on Film: A Century of Hollywood Art Direction* (It Books, 2010)

Pells, Richard, *Modernist America: Art, Music, Movies, and the Globalization of American Culture* (Yale University Press, 2012)

In Invitation

With a view to future revisions, suggestions for additions, corrections of errors, or changes in biographical data are invited.

The publishers cordially invite you to submit your criticisms of this book and any other volumes that bear the History Company name. Ideas for new books or reprints to be added to our catalogue are also most welcome.

Please address your criticisms, corrections, or suggestions to:
support@historycompany.com